LIFELINES

LIFELINES

Poems by
Linda Spock

Antrim House
Bloomfield, Connecticut

Copyright © 2019 by Linda Spock

Except for short selections reprinted for purposes of
book review, all reproduction rights are reserved.
Requests for permission to replicate should
be addressed to the publisher.

ISBN: 978-1-943826-53-7

First Edition, 2019

Printed & bound by Ingram Content Group

Book design by Rennie McQuilkin

Front cover artwork by Getty Images

Author photograph by Ben Blankenburg

Antrim House
860.217.0023
AntrimHouseBooks@gmail.com
www.AntrimHouseBooks.com
400 Seabury Dr., #5196, Bloomfield, CT 06002

For Wayne, who is at the heart of it all.

Acknowledgments

Without the Sunken Garden Poetry Festival in Farmington, CT, I would never have known the beauty and joy of poetry. Thanks to everyone who makes that festival possible.

I wish to thank Vivian Shipley for encouraging me to submit my poetry for publication and getting me started on a path of writing. Thanks to Tony Fusco for publishing my work, "Near Death Experience" in *Caduceus*, a publication of Yale Medical Group Art Place, New Haven, CT. Also, thanks to the Spiritual Life Center in West Hartford, CT for publishing "Spider Woman" in their June 2018 newsletter.

My deepest gratitude to Chivas Sandage for her invaluable mentoring. Her sensitivity, perceptiveness, insight, and constructive feedback helped in the revision of several of the poems in this collection. The members of her writing group were creative sources of inspiration.

My sincere thanks also goes to Blaise Allen, Ph.D., Director of Community Outreach for the Palm Beach Poetry Festival for her ongoing efforts to bring together people who appreciate poetry. The Bards of a Feather Group at Green Cay has listened attentively to my poetry and their enthusiasm is contagious.

Thanks to Elizabeth Pierce and Leah Moore for their friendship and ongoing belief that I had something to say.

Special thanks to Rennie McQuilkin of Antrim House for giving my voice a chance to be heard. His expert editing, artistic vision, and genuine kindness made it a pleasure to experience this new endeavor.

I extend my deepest love and gratitude to my sons, Christopher and Gregory, for allowing me to know the overwhelming happiness that comes from loving unconditionally. Also, thanks to their wives, Angela and Janna, for widening the circle of our family's love, and to Landon and Austin, my precious grandsons, who by their very presence, make the world a better place.

Thanks to my mother, Rose Ciricillo, who gave me her unwavering love and devotion and who always believed in me.

Most importantly, my deepest gratitude to my beloved husband, Wayne Spock who has helped to shape the essence of my heart and soul and whose love provides everything I could ever want. He has read every word, and offered honest insights as only my soulmate and best friend could do. There will never be enough words to thank him.

Table of Contents

I.

Intimate Stranger / 1
Family Reunion / 3
Forcing Orchids / 4
Phantom Limb / 6
Hair / 7
Birthday Wishes / 8
Deciding to Move / 9
The Wedding / 10

II.

Anticipation / 13
Beginnings / 14
Nursery in Moonlight / 15
Test of Faith / 16
Born / 17
Heir Apparent / 18
Baby Giggles / 19
Melt / 20
Radiance / 21
Busy Body / 22
Quick Study / 23
Through Your Eyes / 24
Brazilian Beats / 25

III.

Little Book of Saints / 29
Spider Woman / 30

Prayer While Mopping the Kitchen Floor / 31
My Mind at Night / 32
Hydrangeas in the Snow / 33
Dark Eyes / 34
Erasing Time / 35
Recipe for Living / 36

About the Author / 37
About the Book / 38

LIFELINES

I.

Intimate Stranger

Family legend tells of my grandmother
in a dark house dress
reeling clothes in on a clothesline so firemen did not stare
at her freshly washed underwear

Some days she would interrogate neighbors about their favorite color
having decided if they liked yellow they were not to be trusted

She would stare blankly at them with arms crossed
sitting like a Buddha in the living room

She did not get out of bed or wash herself
but she would cut her toe nails when least expected
leaving a trail of yellowed crescents on the floor

For her to leave her room
she had to be pried loose from her comfort zone
clutching the door frame holding on for dear life to all she had left

After tearing the clothes in her closet barehanded
her brain had to be zapped
cold electrodes causing shock waves to break apart memories of an
18 year old son with movie star good looks killed at war
soon after her husband had died suddenly

Her son's letters and purple heart were all that remained
filling one box left in the attic

Yet, she would endlessly play children's records for me
on a tiny plastic phonograph while I twirled and danced
in my pink tulle dress and gold bangle bracelet
transporting her to a simpler time

My parents' marriage could not survive
under the weight of her pain
My mother did not want to remove
the wedding ring from her finger while
my father wore a new one given to him by another

Somehow I am left
carrying my grandmother's unclaimed suitcase
a family heirloom I would gladly part with

Family Reunion

We all have the same noses
and like the same food
Your house is decorated in blue and white
So is mine
I learn that my brother has grandma's rocking chair
Cousin Fran has grandpa's piano stool
I have grandpa's top hat
and grandma's tea pot
The gypsies took the rest of the stuff
in grandpa's garage

Disconnected yet connected
not having seen each other in many years
we talk and laugh
look at photos of people we've never met
and will never know
skimming highlights of our lives like cream
playing with the puppy in the living room
who shows us how to be
loving to everyone
familiar or not

feeling each other out
to find common ground
on which to balance many years of absence
from one another's lives

so we can have our fill
of family history to sustain us
until someday we can meet again

Forcing Orchids

The perky white flowers of the Dendrobium orchid
peered their heads curiously over the edge of the
gift bag cinched with grograin ribbon

Delicate blossoms attached to spindly stems spiraled skyward
like baby birds open mouthed and hungry
This Mother's Day gift was chosen by my youngest son

The instructions suggested placing the plant in a warm location
with bright filtered light
watering only when needed

Wanting to be sure the plant flourished my son included a book
called *Easy Orchids – Simple Secrets for Glorious Gardens*
It cautioned that in the wild Dendrobiums need protection
from rainstorms which can damage developing buds

Six years later the plant has yet to produce a single flower
The original blooms dropped off
within months and no new shoots appeared

Despite tender coaxing the plant remains flowerless
The shiny leaves seem healthy enough yet refuse to send forth
more fragrant stars

The clay pot's dish is cracked from moisture and time
Still I would not dream of disrupting the
home my plant has known

I hope patience forbearance and faith
will one day send another
fragile burst from the woody stem
But if not I will treasure and remember
the gifts the plant has already given

Phantom Limb

We walk along the jagged coast of Maine arm in arm
you and I
dissecting memories torn from our past
plotting our future

I ask you how is it possible
that even when our boys are grown men
we carry them with us
continually strapped to our backs papoose style
freeze framed

instantly recognizing what they would
notice even when they are not here to see it

They converse by proxy in absentia
unable to utter their lines
yet we know what they would say

When we savored they devoured
their appetites voracious for each moment
in their space
at the cobalt ocean's fractured edge

Their imaginations were architects of sand creations
never to be built again
our rehab for learning to stay in motion
found in the glowing embers of burnished sun

Painkillers are not included for the unrelenting ache

Hair

A pile of contradictions
my curls are either hated or loved
There is no grey zone
except at its roots
Considered beautiful by some
bushy by others
there are only bad hair days
or crowning glory days
Unmanageable yet free
with a mind of its own
defying the smoothness of convention
as tangled and complex as my soul
sometimes requiring no care
yet often demanding special treatment
patiently waiting for self acceptance and gratitude
for my uniqueness

Birthday Wishes

This year
when I blow out the candles
on my cake
I will snuff out bad memories
of your forgetting each of my birthdays
since age eight

It will be the last time
I unwrap the gift of shame
which arrived when friends asked
Where's your father

I will tie up each of the anniversary ghosts
with bright curling ribbon
intent on coiling back on
itself in useless circles

Maybe by next year
Happy Birthday will be
simply that

Deciding to Move

Stormy space no longer shelters me
Friends will be leaving soon
Pilates class is not enough to stretch me
My mind needs daily doses of meditation to soothe the disquiet

Lacking sunshine and warmth
I am tired of bone chilling aches
too much t.v. and wine and sugar
eating out of boredom rather than hunger

I want out

Seeing a For Sale sign will let me know my escape is near
The question becomes where to go
Following adult children will leave me uprooting myself every year
I will miss my dining room table
even though the good china only gets used a few times a year

I am weighed down by too many treasures
My mother's Iladro figurines
my mother-in-law's jade fruit
damask tablecloths and lace cocktail napkins
photographs of people I don't even know
clip on rhinestone earrings and no where to go
record albums collected by my grandfather
each weighing a few pounds
arias sung by Italian tenors with no phonograph to hear them
wedding gifts chosen by our parents' friends of another era
silver candlelabras and candy dishes and crystal decanters
keep me from freedom

I could be in LaJolla

The Wedding

I knew I had to let you go the minute I first saw your face
It has taken me your life to get ready for this
Now it has happened and I have survived

You slept on a foldout bed in our room your last night of single life
just as you started out
a full circle moment before your new life

Admiring you in your white tuxedo jacket
your dark perfect hair
tall and stately awaiting your walk down the aisle
your father and I held your hands
and you agreed to walk with us

My hand trembling in yours
you squeezed it tightly
letting me know it was going to be okay

I teetered on my stilettos seldom worn
the hem of my gown rustling against the fragrant bushes
lining the pathway

Brilliant blue sea and sky
welcomed you to the hydrangea covered trellis where you would
greet your bride

II.

Anticipation

Joy seeps in slowly through the cracks of our lives
while we wait for your new skin and bone to mesh and
your soft flesh to inflate with spongy cells

Hazy sonograms of your shapeless face
stretch us to use our imagination
You, little one, suck your thumb for comfort
as you grow stronger and more human
all the while we grow weaker and more frail

Your spirit takes on form and shape
We remember we have souls and remind ourselves not to cling
to our bodies ready to abandon us

Tiny sneakers and kelly green sunglasses wait for you
Small colorful balls of socks and polka dot bandana bibs are
stacked neatly in your drawer

Your father practices rocking in a chair that will become yours
Your mother plays Mozart for you
calling your name to gently awaken you each morning
trying to touch you through the membrane barrier barely
separating you from her

Miniature seagulls spin above your crib
wondering just like us when you will arrive

Beginnings

Precious pink-skinned bundle of love
hurry up and get here
Not too soon mind you
as you need time to grow
yourself human

I wait to wrap you in warm embrace and
swaddle you with safety
I will comfort your small whimpers
rock you in the sunshine
sing you to sleep with the lullabies I sang
to your father

take you into a world
so large that you will
want to see more

speak sounds you have not heard
until they begin to make sense
to your small ears

You are only a dot of life now
but I will be patient
until you grow arms and legs and eyes

Yet a beating heart exists
within the speck of Spock
I will call my own

Nursery in Moonlight

If I walk into your room at nighttime there will be a pale silvery
glow shimmering through your window shining brightly on the
driftwood crib where you will dream on buttery sheets

I will know it is your room by the scent of love filling the air
as fragrant as peonies and as gentle as violets

There will be no mistaking this room for anyone else's
The miniature leather sandals perched on a tiny twig table will
give it away since they are the ones your father wore

Books line shelves hoping they will be first to be read to you
each one hand-inscribed by someone selecting it with you in mind

The downy comfort of a linen-cushioned rocking chair and warmth
of oaken floors topped with creamy carpet
will be where you learn to walk and talk and sing

Morning will be here soon
but the stars will still be there even when we cannot see them
whispering your name

Test of Faith

We've got this
came through on a whisper cloud in the dead of night
first faintly, then louder
so I would hear its voice and go back to bed

Next it sang its way to me via Jennifer Hudson
This time the refrain
I got this was delivered with soul and rhythm

We left before the hurricane
made landfall so you could be born
in a hospital rather than the back seat
of your father's car

No room at the inns
yet somehow we found shelter in St. Petersburg
Ho Jo's never looked so inviting
as you took your time arriving

Next day we wandered through
a museum admiring Dali
feasting on layered images invading our senses
calming our jangled insides

Pumpkin waffles
grilled watermelon and fried clams –
we ate it all letting ourselves go
knowing *We've got this*

Born

Passing through celestial stardust on gossamer wings
moondust still on your translucent skin
you arrive

Leaving the murky darkness of a watery world
tethered to filament fine as silk yet strong as rope
you leave behind the swirling stillness
to be greeted by the shock of daylight and symphony of sound

Packed like freight in a fleshy cushion
you are now unwrapped
no longer buffered by a cage of rib and feathery tissue

opening a rose bud mouth to breathe in air
your first cry reminding your pulsating heart
to keep beating

Heir Apparent

"I see you"
I tell you whenever we are together

Sometimes I say it in my
sing songy voice but you know I mean it

Beautiful smiling boy
with the downy hair and grey-brown eyes
the sweetness of you seeps through
your porcelain skin
and I see it

When you look back
I believe I have known you forever

Baby Giggles

You surprised yourself
with the sound of your own laugh
It shocked you that it got
such a reception and you wanted to see
if it would happen again

Like clockwork
when grandpa scrolled his spider fingers
over to your side of the table top you roared
as did we your audience and fan club
A royal puppetmaster you pull
the strings of our hearts

When I rocked you to sleep you opened your eyes
and let out a giggle
so I too would laugh before you relinquished
your strangle-hold on the world

your idea of a joke
the punchline shared
by only the two of us

Melt

Your warm body molded itself
against the pillowy folds of my chest
our hearts touching

With powder puff breath you exhaled wisps of air
so delicate it was hard to tell if you were still breathing
except for the gentle rise and fall of your tiny body

It was a zen moment when time ceased to exist
yet all that ever mattered came into clear view
Only love can create the stillness we shared
for that brief moment in time

As Diana Krall sang in the background we swayed
with tears moistening my cheeks
one of which found its way to you

Radiance

When you smile your body comes along for the ride
Your tiny feet and arms start flailing as you become
possessed by sheer delight

It could be as simple as a new sound or color
of a toy dangled in front of you
or the light filtering in from the living room window

When the ceiling fan blade moves ever so slightly
it catches your eye and you become captivated
as if you've just found your beloved

What must it be like to discover what is out there
for the first time full of wonder and adventure and possibility
Of course you don't want a nap . . . but I do

Busy Body

Boy you sure are busy
moving from snatching the tv remote
to investigating the living room shutters

prying open your father's mouth to see how it works
then on to climbing the glass floor lamp
next to the comfortable chair

Pillows piled high on the couch
become your personal Mt. Everest
the topiary trees in pots your forest

Grabbing drawer pulls
opening doors
banging on tables with
all manner of objects
you are on a daily expedition of discovery
while we scurry around you
hoping we can save you from yourself

Quick Study

How is it that in just 5 short months
you already know you want to gum Sophie the giraffe
instead of the red ball

You know sitting up is better than lying down
when you're not tired
and that moving about in your walking car is more fun
than being still

Your taste buds already know
smashed banana is more delicious
than broccoli and carrots

How did you learn so much
about what you want
when I'm still learning how to decide what shoes I like
and it takes me so many more words
to make myself clear

Through Your Eyes

I want to see the world again
through your eyes
open and wide awake
fresh with wonder
as you notice what others miss

I will follow you to a field of soft grass and watch you
find the small pink pebble hiding in plain view
beneath the blades of green
roll it between your baby fingers and try to taste it

I promise to pause with you
to look at spilled coffee on the sidewalk
chewing gum stuck to trees
and paper cups rolling down a path
We will stop and listen to the serenade of blowing palms
and we will allow ice cream to drip deliciously from our lips

In your laboratory of life we will decide if pears squish more
easily than ripened peaches

It will be impossible to tell teacher from pupil

Brazilian Beats

It happened by accident
that I discovered you liked
dancing the samba as much as I do

I left my post at the counter
where I was making a sandwich
to sing to you
You were holding the padded
handrail of your portacrib
listening

Then it happened

Both of us swept up in the drum beats
swaying in synchrony
bopping up and down to the intoxicating rhythm
filling our hearts

You answered the sound of my voice
by flashing your two-teeth grin
then bent your tiny knees in time to the music

I clapped my hands
you chewed on your toys in between waving your arms
I snapped my fingers
you hummed
I shook my hair
you moved your head side to side

Sergio Mendes on vocals
you and I on back up
A perfectly dizzying spectacle
for your grandfather to watch until the happy frenzy
came to a stop

III.

Little Book of Saints

Each night before going to sleep
I would read about another heroine
one of God's chosen girls

Some children dream of being teachers
or astronauts or doctors
I wanted to be a saint

Not sure how to go about it
I imitated the girl next door
who became a nun

I made an altar to Saint Mary
in my bedroom and picked fresh
lily of the valley from my mother's garden

I prayed
got straight As
kept my room neat
listened to my mother
took good care of my brother

all the while knowing
it was going to require much more

I had no visions
I was not a martyr
I performed no miracles
and I wondered continually if being a good girl
would be good enough

Spider Woman

Open like a spider web waiting to
catch a fly
or dandelion wisps
or specks of dirt
is how I want to live my life

not knowing what will come good or bad
big or small
yet still willing to take the time to spin gossamer silk threads
all day if necessary
patiently waiting to see what arrives

One swipe of a broom
can brush the web into oblivion
and yet the spider is willing to take that chance

artfully toiling away creating intricate designs
each one with a unique blueprint all its own

sometimes blending in
not even visible to the human eye seemingly fragile
yet surprisingly strong

Winds do not blow the web away
for the spider knows how to make it
dance rather than break

Prayer While Mopping the Kitchen Floor

Help me find the way back
my soul said
while my purple rubber gloves followed
the push and pull movement of the mop

Eyes inspecting the blackened grout
with crumbs and strands of hair
showcased against the cool white tile
did not keep my heart from asking for directions

My Mind at Night

Tumbleweed of thoughts gathering speed
flailing like feathers flying from an overstuffed pillow
each one floating zig zag

ideas shaken loose in this snowglobe mind
refuse to be still
despite deep breathing or mantras

Questions colliding with answers
stream of consciousness forgetting where it began
leaping wildly in free form fashion with utter abandon
in random chaotic design

Hydrangeas in the Snow

I.

One by one they appeared at my back door
hydrangeas stuck in the snow
mysterious gifts sent by a stranger

I had asked for a sign
when the hydrangeas came
like a steady rain
dried blossoms of curled antique lace
in the vast solitude of an interminable winter
each appearing in the same spot
in case I had not noticed the one before
confirming the answer to my call for grace
reminding me we are not alone

II.

Preserved in beauty
yet withered and fragile
how long will they last before crumbling
Set within the crystal vase
it may be longer
than if left adrift in snow to tumble

Miracle of mine
sacred answers sent
reminds me to trust in faith

Dark Eyes

They say eyes can reveal much about a person
Yours are accepting and loving showing
compassion and gentleness of spirit
as well as quickness of mind and of humor

I want to memorize the lines around your eyes
and hope that I have helped to create more of
the creases caused by smiling and laughing
than the ones etched by hardship and sun

The dark chocolate centers of your eyes
have a way of peering into my soul
illuminating uncharted corners and exposing crevices
Somehow you help me find spaces I did not know existed
in me and in you

Feeling uncovered in this way is different
from trying to sleep on a cold night
when the heavy quilt slides away

Time has confirmed what
my heart recognized instantly at first sight

Erasing Time

Under the glare of sunlight
her beauty faded away
ever so slowly

One strand at a time
the color went
from brown to amber to honey to white

The pink blush of rose
embedded in her skin
became papery white
not wanting the gray of her hair to
feel out of place

Fleshy softness puddled in limp pools
of muscle and bone
settling in places
where hardness had been

Melting her heart along the way
the sharpness of edges dissolved
leaving curves and softness
for compassion to collect

Streams of light
filtered through the cracks
filling interior spaces once dark
erasing remnants of sorrow
bleaching everything white

Recipe for Living

When the sugar coating
falls off the cookie
don't try and put it back on
It is better to eat the cookie
as it is

Try not to complain about its
lack of sweetness
Enjoy it anyway
savoring each morsel
crumbs and all

Linda Spock was a resident of Connecticut for forty-two years before moving to Florida in 2014. She has a doctorate in clinical psychology and was a practicing psychologist for thirty-five years. She considers being a poet a new calling as she feels inspired to write with compassion about the collective human experience with its struggles and triumphs. Her first published poem appeared in *Caduceus,* a publication of Yale Medical Group. This collection is her first book.

Linda has been married for forty-five years and has two married sons who each have a son. Family and writing have been her constant lifelines.

This book is set in Garamond Premier Pro, which had its genesis in 1988 when type-designer Robert Slimbach visited the Plantin-Moretus Museum in Antwerp, Belgium, to study its collection of Claude Garamond's metal punches and typefaces. During the mid-fifteen hundreds, Garamond—a Parisian punch-cutter—produced a refined array of book types that combined an unprecedented degree of balance and elegance, for centuries standing as the pinnacle of beauty and practicality in type-founding. Slimbach has created an entirely new interpretation based on Garamond's designs and on compatible italics cut by Robert Granjon, Garamond's contemporary.

Additional copies of this
book can be ordered at all bookstores.

•

Please visit www.AntrimHouseBooks.com
for information on Antrim House books as well as
sample poems, upcoming events, and a "seminar room"
featuring supplemental biography, notes, images, poems, reviews,
and writing suggestions.

www.ingramcontent.com/pod-product-compliance
Lightning Source LLC
Chambersburg PA
CBHW030134100526
44591CB00009B/655